MW01130858

BRITANNICA BEGINNER BIOS

ROSA PARKS
HEROINE OF THE CIVIL RIGHTS MOVEMENT

THERESE SHEA

Britannica®
Educational Publishing

IN ASSOCIATION WITH

ROSEN
EDUCATIONAL SERVICES

Published in 2015 by Britannica Educational Publishing (a trademark of Encyclopædia Britannica, Inc.) in association with The Rosen Publishing Group, Inc. 29 East 21st Street, New York, NY 10010

Distributed exclusively by Rosen Publishing.
To see additional Britannica Educational Publishing titles, go to rosenpublishing.com.

First Edition

Britannica Educational Publishing
J. E. Luebering: Director, Core Reference Group
Mary Rose McCudden: Editor, Britannica Student Encyclopedia

Rosen Publishing
Hope Lourie Killcoyne: Executive Editor
Christine Poolos: Editor
Nelson Sá: Art Director
Brian Garvey: Designer
Cindy Reiman: Photography Manager

Library of Congress Cataloging-in-Publication Data

Shea, Therese.
Rosa Parks/Therese Shea.
    pages cm.—(Britannica beginner bios)
Includes bibliographical references and index.
ISBN 978-1-62275-697-1 (library bound) — ISBN 978-1-62275-698-8 (pbk.) — ISBN 978-1-62275-699-5 (6-pack)
1. Parks, Rosa, 1913–2005—Juvenile literature. 2. African American women—Alabama—Montgomery—Biography—Juvenile literature. 3. African Americans—Alabama—Montgomery—Biography—Juvenile literature. 4. Civil rights workers—Alabama—Montgomery—Biography—Juvenile literature. 5. African Americans—Civil rights—Alabama—Montgomery—History—20th century—Juvenile literature. 6. Segregation in transportation—Alabama—Montgomery—History—20th century—Juvenile literature. 7. Montgomery (Ala.)—Race relations—Juvenile literature. 8. Montgomery (Ala.)—Biography—Juvenile literature. I. Title.
F334.M753P38667 2015
323.092—dc23
[B]
                                                                              201401333

Manufactured in the United States of America

CONTENTS

CHAPTER ONE

AN INSPIRING ACTION

In December 1955, Rosa Parks refused to give up her seat on a bus in Montgomery, Alabama. Her simple action was very important to the **CIVIL RIGHTS** movement in the United States. Parks was not a powerful or famous person at that time. However, she was brave and demanded to be treated fairly.

Rosa Parks was African American.

> ## Vocabulary Box
>
> The rights of a country's citizens are called CIVIL RIGHTS. They include the right to vote and the right to have an education.

Rosa Parks was a quiet woman who made a brave choice in 1955.

She grew up in a time and place in which racism divided blacks and whites. Blacks were not treated

Quick Fact

For about 100 years after the end of slavery, many African Americans were still treated unfairly. In the 1950s and 1960s, that began to change as African Americans fought for equal rights. This is known as the civil rights movement.

the same as whites. There were even laws that made this unfair treatment legal. Parks believed things could get better. Her small action, refusing to give up her bus seat, was the beginning of great waves of change that spread throughout the United States. Rosa Parks's story is one that continues to inspire people to try to change the world for the better.

CHAPTER TWO

GROWING UP IN ALABAMA

Rosa learned about racism at a young age while growing up in the South.

Rosa Parks was born Rosa Louise McCauley on February 4, 1913, in Tuskegee, Alabama. When she was very young, Rosa, her mother, and her brother moved to Pine Level, Alabama. They lived on a farm owned by Rosa's grandparents. Her grandparents told her what they remembered about slavery. Rosa saw that blacks still did not have the freedom that whites had, even years after slavery had ended.

As a child, Rosa learned about racism. Her grandfather guarded their house with a shotgun to protect the family from the Ku Klux Klan. The Ku Klux Klan was a group of whites who thought that white people were better than blacks. They burned African

When Rosa was growing up, many blacks in the South lived and worked on small farms.

Quick Fact

The Ku Klux Klan was a group that thought that blacks were not equal to whites. They wore white robes and hoods. They did things to scare and hurt African Americans.

American churches. They beat up and even killed blacks.

Rosa learned about **SEGREGATION**, too. White students and black students had to attend different schools. Schools for white

The Ku Klux Klan used burning crosses to scare people.

Vocabulary Box

SEGREGATION is the forced separation of races or classes.

students were much nicer than schools for black students. Whites also went to school for nine months each year. Black students went for only five months so they could work on family farms.

Rosa went to the Montgomery Industrial School for Girls when she was eleven. She continued her

Rosa Parks went to a school much like this one. Blacks and whites did not attend school together where she lived.

Quick Fact

"Negro" and "colored" are two words that were once used to label African Americans. Now many people think these words are rude or mean.

education until the 11th grade. At that point, her grandmother became sick, and Rosa had to leave school to care for her. After her grandmother died, Rosa began to work at a shirt factory in Montgomery. She then went back to school until her mother became sick. She then had to quit school again.

Rosa is shown here at work for a clothing company.

CHAPTER THREE

LIFE IN MONTGOMERY

In 1932, Rosa married Raymond Parks. He was a barber. Raymond wanted Rosa to complete high school. She received her diploma in 1933. It was a proud moment. Only about seven out of one hundred African Americans completed high school at that time, Rosa wrote in her **AUTOBIOGRAPHY**.

Raymond Parks was a member of the National Association for the Advancement of

Vocabulary Box

An **AUTOBIOGRAPHY** is a book someone writes about his or her own life.

Colored People (NAACP). The NAACP worked to make life better for African Americans. Rosa Parks became a member of the NAACP in Montgomery in 1943.

Rosa Parks became a valued member of the NAACP in Montgomery.

Life in Montgomery, Alabama, was hard for African Americans. Both Raymond and Rosa Parks knew it was important to vote so they could choose leaders who would help blacks. However, African Americans had to take a test before they could vote. Rosa Parks took it three times before she was told she passed. She also had to pay money called a poll tax.

One of Montgomery's laws made it illegal for blacks to sit in the first four rows on a public bus. Even if the seats were empty, African Americans could not sit there. They had to sit in the back of the bus. If the bus was full, blacks had to give up their seats to white riders.

Blacks also had to pay at the front of the bus, then get off the bus and enter again through the rear door. In 1943, Rosa Parks was kicked off a bus because she entered at the front and did not get off to reenter at the back. She did this because the back

Blacks and whites were separated on buses in many southern states.

door was crowded with people. Still, the driver forced her off the bus.

On December 1, 1955, Rosa Parks was riding a crowded bus on her way home from work. She was

Quick Fact
The bus driver who forced Rosa Parks off the bus in 1943 was the same driver who had her arrested in 1955.

Parks was fingerprinted after she was arrested.

sitting in the middle of the bus, behind the white rows. When white people got on, the driver told her and others to give up their seats. Parks refused. Parks

This is the picture that the police took of Parks after her arrest.

was arrested and put in jail. People were angry when they heard what happened. They

Vocabulary Box

To BOYCOTT means to refuse to deal with a person or business in order to force them to change.

decided to BOYCOTT the Montgomery buses.

17

CHAPTER FOUR

THE BUS BOYCOTT

Word of Rosa Parks's arrest spread quickly in Montgomery. The NAACP asked black people in Montgomery to stop riding the buses. The NAACP hoped the bus company would be forced to change its rules when it lost money from black riders.

The sidewalks of Montgomery were crowded with people walking to work during the boycott.

Quick Fact

Rosa Parks was not the first black person arrested for refusing to give up her seat on a bus. Claudette Colvin, a 15-year-old girl, was arrested on March 2, 1955, for the same reason.

Martin Luther King Jr. stands in front of a bus during the boycott he had helped organize.

African American leaders formed a new group, the Montgomery Improvement Association (MIA) to oversee the boycott. A man named Martin Luther King Jr. was chosen as its president.

Even people from outside the city gave money so cars could be bought to help blacks in Montgomery.

The group gave demands to the bus company. The MIA wanted the company to hire black drivers. They also wanted people to be allowed to sit in any bus seat. The bus company refused. The MIA decided the bus boycott would continue.

During the boycott, the African Americans of Montgomery worked together. Churches bought large cars and drove people where they needed to go. People also hitchhiked, biked, and walked to work.

The boycott made some white people angry. Many blacks, including Parks, lost their jobs. White people who helped blacks were bullied. People called

Other cities began to protest bus segregation. These people marched in Jackson, Tennessee.

Parks's home and threatened her life. The homes of Martin Luther King Jr. and other black leaders were even bombed.

The NAACP and MIA brought a court case against the city of Montgomery. The case called for the end of segregation on the buses. Their case went to the U.S. Supreme Court, the highest court in the country.

Blacks and whites rode the bus together again after the Supreme Court ordered an end to bus segregation in Montgomery.

On November 13, 1956, the Supreme Court decided that the **U.S. CONSTITUTION** made bus segregation illegal. The boycott ended on December 20, 1956. It had lasted 381 days.

> **Vocabulary Box**
>
> The **U.S. CONSTITUTION** is the official set of laws for the country.

The success of the boycott gave people hope that all kinds of segregation could end peacefully. Martin Luther King Jr. became a well-known leader of the civil rights movement. For her role, Rosa Parks became known as the "mother of the civil rights movement."

CHAPTER FIVE

REMEMBERING ROSA PARKS

Change did not come easily to Montgomery, Alabama. Gunshots were fired at buses. Churches and houses were bombed. Rosa and Raymond Parks continued to receive threatening phone calls. So the Parks family moved to

Parks became a popular speaker at events to end all kinds of segregation and racism.

Detroit, Michigan, in 1957.

Rosa Parks traveled around the United States giving talks about the boycott and the civil rights movement. She went to a

Martin Luther King Jr. inspired many people in Washington, D.C., and around the nation in 1963.

gathering called the March on Washington in 1963. There, Martin Luther King Jr. gave a famous speech known as the "I Have a Dream" speech. Parks was one of the women honored that day.

In 1964, the Civil Rights Act was passed. This law made it illegal to treat people differently because of their race. It ended segregation in schools and other public areas. The Voting Rights Act of 1965 ended **DISCRIMINATION** in voting.

In 1965, Rosa Parks began working for Congressman John Conyers Jr. She did office work and helped homeless people find housing. In 1987, Parks began the Rosa and Raymond Parks Institute for Self Development. This

Vocabulary Box
DISCRIMINATION is the act of treating people unfairly because of their race or beliefs.

group helps educate young people and teaches them to be leaders. Parks also wrote a book for young people called *Rosa Parks: My Story*. The book came out in 1992.

Rosa Parks died on October 24, 2005, in Detroit, Michigan. She was 92. About 50,000 people paid their respects to her coffin in Washington, D.C.

Parks received many honors. In the 1990s, she received the Presidential Medal of Freedom and the

President Bill Clinton awarded Rosa Parks the Congressional Gold Medal in 1999.

Quick Fact

In Montgomery, Alabama, the street on which Rosa Parks was arrested is now named Rosa Parks Avenue.

Congressional Gold Medal. These are two of the highest honors someone in the United States can receive. A postage stamp was created to honor what would have been her 100th birthday in 2013.

A statue of Rosa Parks was placed in the U.S. Capitol in 2013. President Barack Obama said, "In a single moment, with the simplest of gestures, she

President Barack Obama stands next to the new statue of Rosa Parks in the Capitol.

helped change America and change the world." Rosa Parks hoped that anyone would do the same. In fact, Parks said she believed peace was a goal that needed the actions of everyone.

TIMELINE

1913: Rosa Parks is born Rosa Louise McCauley on February 4 in Tuskegee, Alabama.

1924: Rosa begins attending the Montgomery Industrial School for Girls.

1932: Rosa marries Raymond Parks, a barber and member of the NAACP.

1933: Rosa finishes high school and receives her diploma.

1943: Rosa becomes a member of the Montgomery NAACP. She is forced off a Montgomery bus for not entering through the back door.

1955: Rosa Parks refuses to give up her seat on a bus on December 1 and is arrested. The Montgomery bus boycott begins on December 5.

1956: The U.S. Supreme Court outlaws bus segregation on November 13. The Montgomery bus boycott ends on December 20.

1957: The Parks family moves to Detroit, Michigan.

1963: Rosa Parks attends and is honored at the March on Washington.

1964: The Civil Rights Act is passed.

1965: The Voting Rights Act is passed.

1968: Martin Luther King Jr. is shot and killed on April 4.

1977: Raymond Parks dies.

1987: Rosa Parks begins the Rosa and Raymond Parks Institute for Self Development.

1992: The book *Rosa Parks: My Story* comes out.

1996: Parks is honored with the Presidential Medal of Freedom.

1999: Parks receives the Congressional Gold Medal.

2005: Rosa Parks dies on October 24 in Detroit, Michigan.

2013: Rosa Parks is the first African American woman honored with a statue in the U.S. Capitol.

GLOSSARY

ARRESTED Taken into custody for breaking a law.

DIPLOMA A document that shows a person has graduated from a school.

GESTURES Movements or actions that express ideas or attitudes.

INJUSTICE Unfair treatment.

INSPIRE To cause someone to want to do something.

OUTLAWED Made illegal.

RACISM Poor treatment because of someone's race.

SLAVERY Condition in which one person is owned by another.

THREATENED Told someone he or she will be harmed in some way.

TRIAL The hearing and judgment of a case in court.

Books

Aretha, David. *The Story of Rosa Parks and the Montgomery Bus Boycott in Photographs*. Berkeley Heights, NJ: Enslow Publishers, 2014.

Gosman, Gillian. *Rosa Parks*. New York, NY: PowerKids Press, 2011.

Jeffrey, Gary. *Rosa Parks and the Montgomery Bus Boycott*. New York, NY: Gareth Stevens Publishing, 2013.

Parks, Rosa, with Jim Haskins. *Rosa Parks*: *My Story*. New York, NY: Dial Books, 1992.

Ridley, Sarah. *Martin Luther King and the Fight for Equality*. North Mankato, MN: Sea to Sea Publications, 2013.

Websites

Because of the changing nature of Internet links, Rosen Publishing has developed an online list of websites related to the subject of this book. This site is updated regularly. Please use this link to access this list:

http://www.rosenlinks.com/BBB/Parks

INDEX